AF580398

Observations & Beyond

This collection, the debut work of
Jheel Parekh Raghunandan,
delves into the intricacies of love,
the delicate threads of marriage,
the complexities of relationships, and the
poignant reflections on life and death.

For my father

Arun Vrajlal Parekh

and my uncle

Jayprakash Vrajlal Parekh

We make

Marriage

Home

Mr & Mrs

Love

Mr & Mrs

Funeral

Ghar

Hope

We learn

Ruh, soul

Dream

Experience

Purpose

Generation

Reader lives many lives

Circle of life and death

Life lessons

My land

Dreadful

We feel

Mornings

Soil

Pain

Gratitude

Sunrise

Hopelessness

Skin

Love

Love is spring

We ask

Life is a race, or is it?

Madness

Life maybe?

Human

Immortal

Peace

Manto, Shakespeare…

We hide

Masked

Guilt

Face

Observations & Beyond

This collection, the debut work of
Jheel Parekh Raghunandan,
delves into the intricacies of love,
the delicate threads of marriage,
the complexities of relationships, and the
poignant reflections on life and death.

We make

He entered the house
Smiled with his eyes,
Looking for me among the rest of his blood
Ah! He spotted and smiled
I was now at home.

- *Marriage*

The bright mornings
Also bring happiness
To birds without nests

- *Home*

He fooled them all
Convinced them with lies
To own me
To ensure my name ended with his
Boy
Did he know
The game of lie
Ended up being the fate
Of me
Forever
I was no more than him
Than his love
Than his lie
My life was him
That's all my existence was

- *Mr and Mrs*

He drank every drop of me

Making me

Thirsty and dry

-Love

Morning rush
His madness and my stress for
Completeness,
Clash.
Wait begins for evening calmness

- Mr & Mrs

Death

An intimate phenomenon

Too much crowd distorts it

-Funeral

This Saturday night
My soul is watching my heart
And the moon is overlooking my home

-Ghar

She ran within her mansion
Breathlessly from one window to other
Each window would weave her story
One window would weave of entry
The other of exit

- Hope

We learn

Don't be so human that you cheat me.

- Ruh, soul

My eyelids shut
My lips are sealed
Is reality so bad
that
I'm stopped from witnessing beyond 12 hours?

- *Dream*

Kind of love
That makes you drown
But teaches you to swim

- *Experience*

I Bend my head & Pray
While my feet touches the ground
I ask for many things I don't ask for other
things
What a beggar that makes me
Ouch!
My soul cries
Choice of demands in my prayers
Makes me question my existence
Dear lord
What a selfish soul that makes me?
Am I questioning my prayer
Or
Am i answering my prayer?

- Purpose

Driving through the lanes
I see a sea of humans
Standing
Waiting
Agonising
Smiling
Talking
And then I see me In my mirror
My eyes are watching them
With utmost curiosity
And I wonder If I am a drop of this human sea
Why do I have pride
Why do I have ego
Why do I behave immortal
What's so special about me
As this Human wave is gonna get washed off
For the next wave to come

- *Generation*

Having access
To over 1000 books
I knew the story of over 1000 lives

- Reader lives many lives

Cleansing my body
Off the mud that stuck on
Not realising
That's going to be my
Permanent home in time to come

- *Circle of life and death*

Ground doesn't recognise
Whether it's a king walking
Or you
Ground will be slippery
Ground will be rough
Ground will be stable
Ground will become a volcano
Just be sure to look down and walk

- Life lessons

That smell
Of my hair
Which gets tangled
Around your face
Every night
That smell
Is what
Keeps me company
When you're away
From dawn to dusk
That smell
Is what
Takes me from one place
To another destination
In what the world calls as dreamland
For me
That smell is not just a dreamland
It is my land
The land which belongs
To only you
And
Me

- My land

And the days have arrived
Where
Innocent are termed as stupid

- Dreadful

We feel

This morning
I saw the sun
Peeping through my drawn curtains
My scattered hair
On the pillow
Told the sun
Another story
Clouds gathered
Covered the sun
And floated away
My curtains
Threw dark light again
They were loyal to me

\- *Mornings*

We feel

Walking all over
Crushing the earth
Giving way for flowers to bloom

- Soil

Poor you,
You must be so naive
To believe
I am the only emotion that exists

- Pain

We feel

Offering Shukraan,
Sunrise to sunset
Tile to tile
Wall to wall
And to everyone who resides
Within my home

- *Gratitude*

Early Sunday morning,
He took his hands & cupped my face
Waiting for my eyes to open

- *Sunrise*

Her bare thighs
Rubbed on the bedspread
This time
She was providing warmth
To the quilt

\- *Skin*

5 pm sun rays
Made my heart sink
Ahead of the sun itself
I had to put to rest
Those finger games
Innocent plays
Where the sun let my hair reflect gold
And his eyes shunned partially
Partially looking at me
Battling the rays
Those eyes pierced right through me
5:13 now, I saw
Walked ahead and draped my shawl
To flaunt the believable image of me
The unreal me
To the world outside of him.

\- *Love*

We feel

I knew
The beast in me
Would deceive me
For his love

- Hopelessness

A bird
landed on a tree stem.
Flowers blossomed on that barren branch
Oh, what a love story that was!

\- *Love is spring*

We ask

We ask

Ahead or behind
Why worry
When the burying is Still

- Life is a race, or is it?

We came so close
And merged
That,
I forgot -
Was I the island
Or
Was I the shore

- *Madness*

We ask

Isn't the process of entering the world
Also a process of death for the baby in the womb?

- Life, maybe?

Running
All my life
To Stand still?

\- *Human*

We ask

Im breathing
Just so that
I don’t stop breathing

- Immortal

For how long
Will you inflate your ego
And
Wait for it to burst?

- *Peace*

We ask

Is it true

Can only a troubled writer

-Write?

- *Manto, Shakespeare, Kafka, Hemmingway,*

Elizabeth Gilbert.....

We hide

Her cold lips
Had cracks when they smiled
Winter, was not her summer

\- *Masked*

We hide

That moment
When what intimated you the most
Comes to embrace you
And you pretend
Like you always had an attitude
To embrace back

- Guilt

The lines on my forehead
Screamed my displeasure
Where's my mask? Where's my mask?

- *Face*

Prepare to immerse yourself in a world
where every emotion finds its voice
- a world within the pages of

Observations & Beyond

www.ingramcontent.com/pod-product-compliance
Lightning Source LLC
LaVergne TN
LVHW090140160826
845673LV00017B/2529
9798892770699